Coffee and Conversation
with Ruth Bell Graham
and Gigi Graham Tchividjian

Coffee and Conversation
with *Ruth Bell Graham*
and *Gigi Graham Tchividjian*

VINE BOOKS
SERVANT PUBLICATIONS
ANN ARBOR, MICHIGAN

© 1997 by Ruth Bell Graham and Gigi Tchividjian
All rights reserved.

Vine Books is an imprint of Servant Publications especially designed to serve evangelical Christians.

Scripture quotations, unless otherwise indicated, are taken from the HOLY BIBLE, NEW INTERNATIONAL VERSION®. © 1973, 1978, 1984 by International Bible Society. Used by permission of Zondervan Publishing House. All rights reserved. Verses marked RSV are from the Revised Standard Version of the Bible, © 1946, 1952, 1971 by the Division of Christian Education of the National Council of Churches of Christ in the USA. Used by permission.

Previously published pieces by Ruth Bell Graham appear courtesy of Baker Book House and Oliver Nelson Publishers.

Published by Servant Publications
P.O. Box 8617
Ann Arbor, Michigan 48107

Photography by: Bob Foran and Gwen Ellis.
Additional photography supplied by Gigi Tchividjian and Ruth Bell Graham.
Cover design: BC Studios, Colorado Springs, CO

97 98 99 00 01   10 9 8 7 6 5 4 3 2 1

Printed in Mexico
ISBN 1-56955-041-7

LIBRARY OF CONGRESS CATALOGING-IN-PUBLICATION DATA

Graham, Ruth Bell.
Coffee and Conversation with Ruth Bell Graham and Gigi Graham Tchividjian.
    p.   cm.
ISBN 1-56955-041-7
1. Graham, Ruth Bell.   2. Baptists—United States—Biography.   3. Graham, Billy, 1918-   Family.   I. Tchividjian,
Gigi.   II. Title.
BX6493.G83   1997
269'.2'0922—dc21
[B]   97-15781
                                                                                                            CIP

Contents

Please Come In

❧ *Gigi* ❧

As the car climbed up the last hill and rounded the last bend, I could see a light on in my bedroom window. It was late when I finally arrived at the old log house up on the mountain.

As I got out of the car, the dogs stirred and glanced up sleepily from their place by the front door. Their tails thumped in lazy recognition and the younger one slowly, reluctantly got up to greet me. I opened the front door. Before I could even put down my luggage, the cat appeared and began rubbing against my legs.

All was quiet. Careful not to make any noise, I went into the kitchen, heated a cup of milk, and tiptoed upstairs to my old room. There I found the bedside lamp on beside a small, colorful bouquet of fresh flowers, my bed turned down, and, on my pillow, a note of warm welcome written in Mother's distinctive hand.

Soon, I was curled up between fresh sheets, happy to be "home" again.

I slept soundly and was awakened in the morning by bright sunshine streaming in through the window. Grabbing my robe, I went quickly and quietly down the stairs to the kitchen, hoping to be the first one up so that I could make the coffee. I like mine strong—probably the influence of Stephan, my European husband who was raised in Switzerland—but other members of the family, notably Daddy, like theirs weak. When I'm home, it's always a race to see who can get to the coffeepot first.

Brewing the first pot of the day, I became aware of the unique fragrance of this beloved room and I was flooded with memories. The old log walls, gently seasoned by years of smoke from the large, open fireplace—Mother won't give two cents for a fireplace that doesn't smoke—and the many meals we had prepared and enjoyed here give this room a special scent all its own.

Once again the cat greeted me at the kitchen door, hoping I would take pity on him and fill his bowl. I filled it, and then I went to light the fire, which had been laid the night before to be all ready to chase away the early morning chill.

While the coffee was brewing, I sat down in front of the window savoring the view of the Blue Ridge Mountains and the fact that I was here—home. So many wonderful memories … so much to be thankful for … so much to share. I was reminded once again that "to whom much is given much shall be required."

My thoughts were interrupted—the sound of sputtering steam alerted me to the fact that the coffee was ready. I poured myself a cup and returned to my seat. Yes, I had been given so much. Sitting in my childhood home, sipping hot coffee in front of the blazing fire, I felt warmed inside and out.

The smoke from the freshly-lit fire, mingled with the rich aroma of the coffee, must have made its way back to Mother's room, because it wasn't long before I heard her footsteps coming down the long hallway.

I jumped up to hug and kiss her and offered her a cup of coffee. Because I had beat her to the coffeepot, she sweetly asked me to add some hot milk to hers.

For the next several hours, we just sat and talked, laughed, and shared. Before we knew it, we had spent the better part of the morning just drinking coffee and talking.

It doesn't matter where we are. In my childhood home in the

mountains of North Carolina, on the balcony of a chalet in Switzerland, on vacation together in the Caribbean, or in my kitchen in Florida, wherever we are, Mother and I enjoy our coffee and conversation. We only wish that you could join us.

Since that is not possible, we invite you to listen in on a few of our times of sharing as you read this book. And if you are ever around, you are more than welcome to come in and have coffee and conversation with us.

A Personal Word

~ *Ruth* ~

When I was a student in a Christian college we enjoyed a guest chapel speaker who brought a challenging and inspiring message.

I hungered for spiritual challenge and inspiration and so was delighted to be invited to sit at the same lunch table with this speaker and other students.

An hour later, I headed back to class. I was very disappointed. The entire lunch time had been spent joking and telling funny stories. Perhaps the speaker thought he was relating well to the students. And he may have been. But there was at least one student who left spiritually hungry.

As you read this book, you may at times chuckle, but I trust that you will not leave our coffee time "hungry" in your soul.

Remembering

~ Gigi ~

The fire crackled cheerily in the large fireplace, bathing my parents' living room in a soft glow. The only other lights were those from the tall Christmas tree that stood by the window. Snowflakes fell silently outside. I sat alone on the brightly polished hearth, hugging my knees and staring into the flames, remembering....

This room with its beamed ceiling, ancient furniture, worn brick floor, and chintz-covered couches held so many memories for me. So much of what I knew of the Lord and the Scripture I learned right here.

Growing up in this house, Sundays were special. Mother woke us with gospel hymns playing on the record player and the smell of sweet rolls in the oven. After church and lunch, we rested, read, or took long walks to the top of the ridge, passing the "bears' den" on the way, or stopping by

the reed field to gather wildflowers. Late in the afternoon my grand-parents would arrive to spend the evening.

Our church did not have evening services, so we would eat a quick sup-per, then light the fire and gather in this room to sing hymns, play Bible games, and share experiences of God's goodness.

With my grandmother at the piano, we sang our favorites from ancient hymns of the church to the popular new choruses. When our voices gave out, each child cuddled up to an adult who coached as we played "Spit in the Ocean" and "Twenty Questions." As the younger children grew sleepy, they were excused one by one and tucked into bed, until only the older ones were left to listen as the adults reminisced.

Daddy might recount an exciting experience of God's faithfulness in his latest crusade, or tell how the Lord had led him in making a difficult deci-sion. My grandfather, a surgeon, might tell how the Lord had touched a patient, bringing not only physical but spiritual healing. Then a Scripture or specific answer to prayer might be shared.

I grew up hearing of God's sovereignty, his constant presence, his protection and mercy, his power and grace, his faithful care and provision of both material and spiritual needs. My parents and grandparents always spoke of the Lord as they would of their best friend. These sessions were not planned but flowed naturally and spontaneously from hearts filled with love and gratitude.

As I sat on the warm hearth recalling all the happy times experienced around this fireplace, I thought about how precious such a Christian heritage is, and how important it is to "remember." We read in Deuteronomy 4:9-10, "Do not forget the things your eyes have seen or let them slip from your heart as long as you live. Teach them to your children and to their children after them. Remember.... "

The Example

~ Gigi ~

Spending the night at my grandparents' house was always a special treat. I was all ready for bed. I grabbed my pillow and my school clothes, ran up our drive, crossed the little wooden bridge, and darted across the street and down into my grandparents' yard. The back porch light was still on, and I knew the door would not be locked.

When I ran in, LaoNaing (Grandmother) not only gave me a hug, but some freshly-baked custard and one of her special mints. I kissed her good night, then circled through the living room to find Lao I (Grandfather). After giving him a kiss, I climbed the stairs to bed.

The small sleeping porch was perched high among the trees. With the bed pushed up against the windows, it was almost like being in a tree house. I loved falling asleep in the soft glow of the full moon.

Though I awoke early, the birds were up before me, singing their hearts out—blue jays, cardinals, thrashers, Carolina chickadees, and, every now and then, a bright yellow-and-black Baltimore oriole or a vivid blue indigo bunting. Sometimes even a pileated woodpecker would drill just outside my window, waking me with a start.

The first rays of sunlight were just beginning to touch the ridge behind the house. I lay there watching as they gradually lit the summit, then slowly slid down the mountain. Before I left for school, the sun would have already reached the valley, warming us with its presence.

I could smell breakfast cooking—bacon, eggs, and hot biscuits! I got up and dressed quickly, then tiptoed down the stairs. When I reached the bottom landing, I peered around the corner into the living room. Yes, he was there as he was every morning, on his knees in front of the big rocking chair. I stood watching him until LaoNaing called us to breakfast. He got up slowly, rubbing his eyes before he replaced his glasses, his forehead still red and creased from the impact of his folded hands. He saw me and smiled. Giving me a warm hug and a big kiss, we went into the kitchen together.

I knew that this active surgeon, church layman, writer, former missionary to China, and family man had been up long before dawn, spending time with the Lord. He had an extensive prayer list, and I felt warm and secure, knowing he had already prayed for me. Now he was refreshed and eager to meet the rest of his busy day.

My grandfather never disappointed me as a man or as a Christian. Until the day he died, he set an example of practical, balanced, fun-loving, disciplined, godly living.

When I examine my own life, I wonder what my children see. Do they see a concern for others, or do they see criticism, cynicism, and compromise? Do the things of eternal and spiritual value have priority in my life, or am I too preoccupied with the material and temporal things? Which is more important—my children's little feet or their footprints? The fun we have eating popcorn together, or the salt and butter on the carpet? Do they discern a sense of peace and serenity in our home, or strife and tension? Do I walk my talk? Is there a noticeable difference in my life? Do they perceive acceptance, love, and understanding? Do they experience the result of my prayers? Is the fruit of the Spirit exemplified in my life?

Anchored to a Sure Rock

Gigi

I am often asked, "What is the most important thing you have learned from your mother?" Although it is a hard question to answer because I have learned so much from her, I would have to say that the two most important things I have learned from her are how to rely totally upon the person of Jesus Christ and the importance of loving the Scriptures.

The Word of God is a living Word; it is the person of Jesus Christ, himself, revealed to us. Psalm 119 says that the Word cleanses, strengthens, delights, teaches, saves, comforts, directs, and gives understanding. What a resource!

I am so grateful that I was taught early in my life to use this resource; to draw strength from it; to use it in seeking direction and guidance; to employ it in times of discouragement, disappointment, and loneliness.

At the age of thirteen, Mother was sent away from China to attend high school in North Korea. She suffered terribly from homesickness. All that she had learned while still living with her parents was put to the test. It was there that the Living Word became a daily resource from which she could draw.

At the age of twelve, I, too, went away to boarding school. I remember so well that awful gnawing feeling of loneliness and homesickness in the pit of my stomach. Instinctively, I turned to the Bible for comfort, because Mother and Daddy had taught me while still very young to turn to the Lord and to his Word for help in every situation. During those weeks and

months I learned many things about the vast resource I had in my personal relationship with the Lord Jesus and his Word. I now look back on those days as a spiritual experience for which I will be eternally grateful.

Since those days there have been many disappointments and heartaches. There have been times of decision and times of discouragement. In each case I have gone to his Word. He has *never once* failed to lift me up.

There may come a day when we will no longer have the written Word of God. It is possible that it will have been taken away from us. But no one will ever be able to take away what we have hidden in our hearts and minds. Even if we do have our printed Bibles to refer to, reciting memorized Scripture is a simple way of abiding in God's Word all during the day.

I have taught my children Bible verses from the time they first began to talk, and it has always amazed me how quickly their minds grasped the words. I myself find memorizing difficult, but I keep trying. I place a much-loved Bible verse or passage on the kitchen counter or on the ironing board. When I'm going to an appointment, I put a verse in my pocket or purse. Then while I wait at a doctor's office or elsewhere, I can take the verse out and work at memorizing it. I even put a verse in the car and repeat it while driving or waiting in traffic.

When Mother Graham, my paternal grandmother, was in her late eighties, I visited her in the hospital. A short time before my visit, her doctor had come to talk with her about her condition, which was very serious. His report made her so upset she couldn't even speak. When the doctor left the room, my grandmother automatically turned to her Lord—the One she had known for so many years—for comfort and strength. She couldn't pick up her Bible to read it, but a Bible verse she had memorized many years before came to her mind and gave her the needed courage and assurance for her stay in the hospital.

Be sure to weave the unfailing threads of God's Word through the fabric of your heart and mind. It will hold strong, even if the rest of life unravels.

This is my ledge
of quiet,
my shelf of peace,
edged
by its crooked rails
holding back the beyond.
Above,
a hawk sails
high
to challenge clouds
trespassing
my plot of sky.
Below
in the valley,
remote and dim,
sounds

come and go,
a requiem
for quiet.
Here on my ledge,
quiet praise:
of birds,
crickets,
breeze—
in different ways;
and so do I—
for these:
my ledge of quiet,
my plot of sky:
for peace.

Ruth

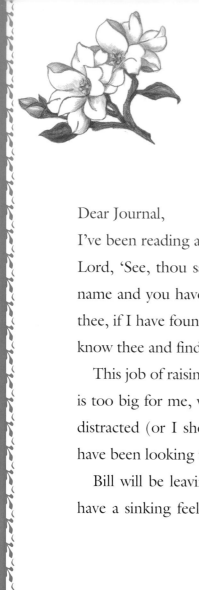

Ruth

Dear Journal,

I've been reading again from Exodus 33:12-16 (KJV): "Moses said to the Lord, 'See, thou sayest to me, "Bring up this people.... I know you by name and you have also found favor in my sight." Now therefore, I pray thee, if I have found favor in thy sight, show me now thy ways, that I may know thee and find favor in thy sight....'"

This job of raising five little Grahams to be good soldiers of Jesus Christ is too big for me, who am not a good soldier myself. Feeling particularly distracted (or I should say overwhelmed and confused) this morning, I have been looking to the Lord asking, "Where, from here?"

Bill will be leaving soon for the San Francisco meeting. And I almost have a sinking feeling. Not altogether a left-behind and left-out sort of feeling, but swamped, knowing that all the things I have depended on others to do, I shall have to do myself.

And things have not been going smoothly. There is a terrible amount of fighting among the children, ugliness and back talk from Gigi, and peevishness on my part backed by sporadic, uncertain discipline. My friend, Mr. Sawyer said, in speaking of his mother the other day, "When she said 'whoa' we knew she meant 'whoa'."

I am not walking the Lord's way at all. I am doing what I feel like doing rather than what I ought to do. These verses hit me hard: "She who is self-indulgent is dead even while she lives" (1 Tim. 5:6, RSV), and "The fruit of the Spirit is ... self-control" (Gal. 5:22, 23).

Self-indulgence is doing what we want rather than what we ought. I had always thought of self-control applying to temper or to drink. But what about the almonds in the pantry, the ice cream and chocolate sauce, the candy which I know will add unnecessary pounds and make my face break out? What about controlling my tongue? My tone of voice?

Standing up straight? Writing letters? All these and many more things need controlling.

And I don't look well to the ways of my household. The children are not well taught even about brushing their teeth and keeping their rooms straight. Regular family prayers at the supper table are not very regular. I don't always keep the children's clothes mended, neat, and organized. We get ready for Sunday on Saturday. Well, there's no use going into it all. It just boils down to the fact that I am not being a good mother.

So I took it to him this morning. I want above everything to be the kind of person he wants. If he had his undisputed way in me, I would be. Everything would solve itself. The place to begin is here, with me. The time to begin is now. And as I reread Exodus 33:12-16, the phrase that I had never noticed before and that now jumped out at me was: "Show me now thy ways."

Sojourner's Rest

～ Ruth ～

Bill was away in Rio de Janeiro addressing the Baptist World Alliance one summer. My job was to pack five little Grahams and myself for a summer in Switzerland. I had offered to go and address the Baptists while he packed and prepared the five little Grahams for Switzerland, but the idea was not received with enthusiasm. Only a mother who has tried to pack her large family for several months in a foreign country will know the difficulty of the job.

Finally, preparations were finished and we climbed aboard a jet headed for Switzerland. After a long and tiring day, the plane landed in Geneva where we were met by our hosts.

I was too tired that night to notice much of anything. I just felt the warmth of our hosts' welcome and the coolness of the linen sheets after the children and I had been tucked safely into our beds.

The next morning when I woke and pulled up the rolling blinds, I found myself looking out over Lake Geneva. The snowcapped mountains beyond the lake rose to the majestic Dents du Midi. Everything was utterly charming and peaceful. That is, until the children awoke!

Keeping house in Europe, I found, was considerably different from keeping house in America. I found a good part of my time was taken up simply in keeping the family fed and the house functioning. Grocery shopping needed to be done every day. Not only that, instead of supermarkets there were small shops for each particular item: a butcher shop, a cheese shop, a grocery store, a fruit stand, and so forth. The bread boy came every day with long, skinny loaves of freshly baked, unwrapped, French bread—crusty on the outside, light and scarce on the inside—sticking out of the basket on the back of his bicycle.

And the result of all this activity? Spiritual drought. For me, spiritual dryness usually results from an extremely busy period. We must be quiet for the Spirit to speak to us, and I was anything but still. Air must be still for dew to fall.

One day, our friends Bob and Myrl Glockner, who were spending the summer nearby, came and collected all five children and our house guest, Dorothy Mayell, Gigi's high school roommate, and took them off for the day.

No sooner were they out of sight than I grabbed my Bible, found an empty chaise in the sun on the portico leading from the dining room to the front yard, and there I read from the book of Job all day. I felt like the prophet Elijah, fed by angels in the desert when he had reached the end of himself. Fed and refreshed, we are told, he went in the strength of that food forty days and forty nights.

Late that afternoon, the car pulled up the drive and through the iron gates. All the occupants piled out. They were tired but happy, full of the day's experiences. Supper was waiting and their mother was refreshed and eager to have them back.

The children are all grown now and much of the time I am alone in this big old log house. It has been many years since I have had to get up in the night with a sick child. I don't have to grocery shop and cook for a crowd. And although I have more time now to read and study, I still experience dry spells. But I have found the principles for curing dryness are the same for me today as they were when all the children were small and still at home. I find that when I am dry, if I will reach for my Bible and spend time alone in his Word … the Living Word … I once again feel fed and refreshed.

The Clearing

❧ Gigi ☙

It was still early. I sat at the dining room table with a cup of hot coffee. Nothing tastes better than that first cup of fresh coffee in the morning!

Sitting in that particular spot brought back a legion of warm memories. It was in this room, as a child, that I ate most of my meals. I had grown up in this cozy little house, and played outside in that very yard.

Nothing much had changed and yet … I recalled everything being so much *larger*. The round dining room table seemed to have dwindled, and the curved window wasn't nearly as large as I remembered. The yard, too, had diminished in size since I used to play dress up and pretend I was Mrs. Vanderbilt from Fort Lauderdale, Florida. My "mansion" had been located securely behind a hedge of thick rhododendron bushes. (I never dreamed that one day Fort Lauderdale would actually be my home.)

A big thunderstorm had passed through the previous night, drenching our cove with heavy rain. The little stream rushed eagerly along as it tumbled over the tiny waterfall my mother had built years ago. A few raindrops still clung to the leaves of overhanging trees and each time the pesky little squirrel, who delighted in stealing the birdseed, jumped from branch to branch, a shower of drops would accompany him.

As I looked out over the familiar yard, I suddenly noticed one major reason why it all seemed so much smaller. *It was.*

The yard of my childhood had been larger—literally. The trees, bushes, and surrounding undergrowth had continued to grow just as I had, and the yard had simply become overgrown.

I grabbed another cup of coffee and quickly went to put on my jeans. Grabbing a rake and a pair of clippers, I launched into my attack. It wasn't until several hours later, discouraged and thoroughly exhausted, that I had to admit the job was bigger than I. All my labors had hardly made a dent!

If the job were to get done, I needed some help.

Soon, my friends David and Greg arrived with tree-climbing boots, a chain saw, and a large chipper. I pointed out the problem and they began to work with a will.

The chain saw whined all day while I went back to my window to sit and watch.

David and Greg pruned, cut, pulled, dragged, sawed, and raked. Brambles, twisted vines, fallen trees, rotten stumps, weeds, undesirable saplings, leaves, and branches, were all removed. It wasn't long before an enormous mound of debris piled up in the middle of the driveway. Then, in just a matter of minutes, the chipper transformed it all into a mound of useful mulch to be spread around the flower beds.

✦

I am the true vine, and my Father is the gardener. He cuts off every branch in me that bears no fruit, while every branch that does bear fruit, he prunes so that it will be even more fruitful.... This is to my Father's glory, that you bear much fruit, showing yourselves to be my disciples.

JOHN 14: 1-2, 8

Good-bye Again

~ Gigi ~

Mother stood waiting outside the doorway.

The suitcases were packed and standing in the hallway, ready to be loaded into the car. We children ran around the driveway, laughing and playing while we waited for Daddy. Suddenly his tall, handsome figure appeared in the doorway, overcoat slung over one arm, hat on his head. We ran to him, dreading what we knew would be another long separation. He took each of us in his strong arms, held us tightly, and then kissed us good-bye.

I couldn't bear to look into his eyes, because I knew they would be glistening with tears. Though there were many such good-byes while we were growing up, it never got easier. We would back away and watch as

Daddy took Mother in his arms, kissing her warmly and firmly, knowing it would be some time before he would hold her again.

Then before we knew it, Daddy was whisked away in the car, around the curves and down the steep mountain drive. We listened to the retreating sound of the engine and waited for the final "toot" of the horn as he reached the gate. Another plane to catch, another city, another crusade, another period of weeks before we would be together as a family once more.

I turned to look at Mother, sensing her feeling of loss and loneliness. Her eyes were bright with unshed tears, but there was a beautiful smile on her face as she said, "Okay, let's clean the attic! Then we'll have LaoNaing and Lao I up for supper! (That's Chinese for maternal grandmother and maternal grandfather. Mother's parents, the Nelson Bells, served for twenty-five years as missionaries to China. They retired to a home only a mile down the mountain from us, and were living there at the time of this parting.)

Not once did my mother make us feel that by staying behind she was sacrificing her life for us children. By her sweet, positive example, her consistently unselfish spirit, and her total reliance upon the person of Jesus Christ, we were kept from bitterness and resentment. We learned, instead, to look for ways to keep busy and prepare for Daddy's homecoming.

Years later, I asked Mother how she had endured so many years of good-byes. She laughed and quoted the old mountain man who had said, "Make the least of all that goes and the most of all that comes."

Laughing, We Endure

We live a time
secure;
beloved and loving,
sure
it cannot last
for long,
then—
the good-byes come
again—again—
like a small death,
the closing of a door.
One learns to live
with pain.

One looks ahead,
not back—
never back
only before.
And joy will come again—
warm and secure,
if only for the now,
laughing
we endure.

Ruth

The Devil Is a Good Devil

❦ *Gigi* ❧

The long antique table was beautifully set with our best silver and china, its highly-polished surface reflecting the warm glow of candlelight. It was unusual for us to be gathered in the dining room for our evening meal. We usually ate supper in the cozy kitchen around the big, circular Lazy-Susan table in front of the fireplace. (Each of us would hold onto the Lazy-Susan and, as soon as the blessing was over, we would see who could be first to spin it. Mother used to say that this prepared us for life in a highly competitive world!) However, since Daddy was home from a crusade, we had decided to celebrate his homecoming.

Daddy said the blessing, ignoring the baby who kept interrupting with his "Amen." Then, minding our manners, we passed the Southern fried chicken, homemade rolls, rice and gravy, and, for dessert, apple pie. How nice it was to be a "complete" family again. How glad we were that Daddy was home.

At mealtime, fun and laughter always abounded, and during dinner someone began to sing a popular chorus.

> *I've got the joy, joy, joy, joy down in my heart*
> *(Where?)*
> *Down in my heart—down in my heart*
> *I've got the joy, joy, joy, joy down in my heart,*
> *Down in my heart to stay.*

> *I've got the love of Jesus, love of Jesus down in my heart.*
> *(Where?)*
> *Down in my heart—down in my heart.*
> *I've got the love of Jesus, love of Jesus down in my heart.*
> *Down in my heart to stay.*

Soon, we all joined in and continued through several more verses, concluding with our favorite:

> *And if the devil doesn't like it, he can sit on a tack.*
> *Sit on a tack—sit on a tack.*
> *And if the devil doesn't like it, he can sit on a tack.*
> *Sit on a tack to stay.*

To our surprise, Daddy looked up with a frown and said a bit sternly, "I don't want you to sing that verse anymore."

We were a bit taken aback, since he was an old softy and tended to spoil us. Turning inquiring eyes on him, we asked why.

"Because," he replied, "the devil is a good devil."

All of us, including mother, burst out laughing. Then we noticed that he looked very serious.

"What I mean," he explained, "is that the devil does a very good job of being a devil, and I think it is wrong to take him lightly or mock him. He is real and powerful, and he is no joking matter."

I sat there pondering what Daddy had said. I didn't understand fully at the time, but I did begin to develop a healthy respect for Satan and the power he wields. And though I have never been afraid of him, knowing I am under the protection of the blood of Jesus, neither have I given him the satisfaction of being preoccupied with him. Following Daddy's advice, I have never touched things associated with Satan's domain. Years later, when the occult and witchcraft became a popular fad, I asked the Lord to help me to be sensitive and discerning concerning these matters whether it be a game, movie, or book and have remembered the lesson learned so long ago around the dinner table.

The Happy Little Cricket

I captured him in Kleenex
and threw him out with care—
the happy little cricket
enlivening the air.
For it was late and I,
tired from the noise of day,
tossed sleepless, then decided my
rest precluded his play.
And so he was moved
without notice: I didn't even wince;
But slept serenely all night long,
… and have missed him
ever since.

Ruth

Solitude, My Companion

⋅ Ruth ⋅

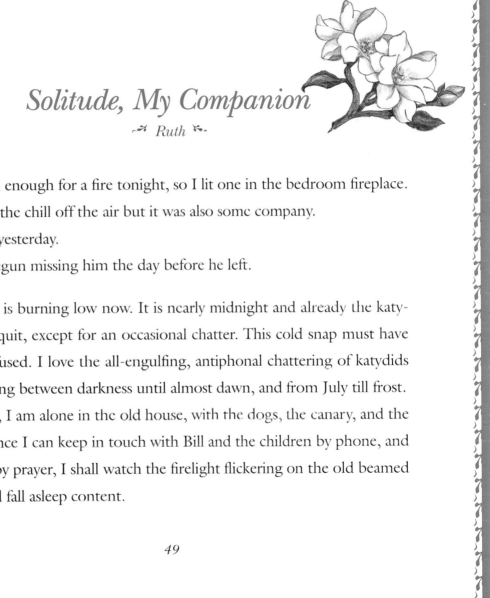

It is cool enough for a fire tonight, so I lit one in the bedroom fireplace. It took the chill off the air but it was also some company.

Bill left yesterday.

I had begun missing him the day before he left.

The fire is burning low now. It is nearly midnight and already the katydids have quit, except for an occasional chatter. This cold snap must have them confused. I love the all-engulfing, antiphonal chattering of katydids each evening between darkness until almost dawn, and from July till frost.

Anyway, I am alone in the old house, with the dogs, the canary, and the cat, and since I can keep in touch with Bill and the children by phone, and the Lord by prayer, I shall watch the firelight flickering on the old beamed ceiling and fall asleep content.

A Big Man

~ Ruth ~

In the winter of 1971, we were spending a few weeks in Florida. Bill joined the family when he could. Gigi and Stephan were flying down to weekend with us and would be landing at Melbourne, the nearest airport.

Bill, busy with another appointment, asked a friend to drive me to the airport.

Another friend had left a suitcase and golf clubs with us and so we were going to take them to the airport to send them to him in North Carolina by air freight.

"Just drop me off with the suitcase and clubs at the entrance," I said to my friend, as the only parking allowed was in the lot just across the street. "I'll get a porter to carry them to air freight for me."

As he drove off, I spotted two young men sitting on a bench near the door.

"Could one of you take these to the air freight counter for me?" I asked.

"Sure," one replied. Securing a cart, he lifted the bags aboard and I followed him to the air freight counter.

There I learned that air freight was closed for the weekend. Just then, my friend walked in. I explained the situation to him and suggested he have the porter put the bags back in the car, adding, "I tipped him on the way in. You tip him on the way out."

While he took care of the matter, I went to the coffee shop to get a cup of coffee.

In a few minutes my friend joined me, chuckling.

"You sure know how to pick 'em!"

"Pick what?" I asked.

"Pick porters," he laughed.

"What do you mean?"

"Well, when we got to the car, I tried to tip the guy and he refused, saying you had already given him too much. I said, 'You don't look like a porter to me,' and he said, 'I'm not.'

"What do you do for a living?" I asked.

"'I pitch for the Minnesota Twins.'"

Still laughing, my friend got up and left the coffee shop. In a few minutes he was back with "the porter."

"Ruth," he said, "I'd like you to meet Al Metz, pitcher for the Minnesota Twins. It takes a big man to be willing to do a little job."

The Same Spirit Says
the Same Thing

~ Gigi ~

I was sitting on the window seat in my bedroom overlooking the Blue Ridge Mountains. The trees were bare and the air so crisp and clear that I could distinctly see all the activity in the valley below. Bright Christmas lights enticing shoppers. Cars winding slowly up the narrow mountain roads. Yellow-and-black school buses, stopping to unload children who were hurrying home to warmth and supper. And, every now and then, a long freight train inching its way lazily across the valley floor. Although I took note of all these familiar sights, my mind was thousands of miles away—high in the Swiss Alps.

In my lap was a letter from a handsome, godly man, six years my senior, who was asking me to marry him and move to Europe. Although I had met him several years earlier, I didn't know him well nor had we had any

53

contact for many months. Yet, somehow, I knew the Lord was directly involved in this proposal. I glanced down and my eyes fell again on the sentence that kept turning over and over in my heart. It read simply: "The same Spirit says the same thing."

As I watched the late afternoon sun slide slowly behind the ridge, I wondered how a naïve, seventeen-year-old girl could make such a momentous decision. I got up and walked to the bedside table where my Bible lay open to Isaiah 1:19: "If ye be willing and obedient, ye shall eat the good of the land" (KJV).

Was I willing? Did I really want God's will more than anything else in my life? Was I willing to be available to him, to trust him, to obey him? Was I willing to follow his leading even if it meant leaving all that was dear and familiar to me and giving myself to a man I didn't yet know well enough to love?

I knew that I had to be able to answer these questions before I could know God's perfect plan for my life.

The days passed, and I continued to search my Bible and my heart.

Then one day, I awoke with a real sense of joy. I knew beyond a shadow of doubt that I could answer a resounding YES to each of those probing questions. Yes, I did want his will more than anything. Yes, I would follow and obey him. Yes, I could trust him. Hadn't he said, "For I know the plans I have for you … plans to prosper you and not to harm you, plans to give you hope and a future" (Jer. 29:11)?

The peace "that passeth understanding" flooded my being that December day, and I knew that the same Spirit that had impressed dear Stephan to ask me to marry him was now assuring me, by faith and not by feeling, to answer yes.…

***

Daddy held my hand ever so tightly as we climbed the steep, winding road to the little church that clung to the side of the mountain overlooking Montreux, Switzerland.

The jonquils nodded their heads approvingly as we passed, and the yellow blossoms of the forsythia seemed to have opened overnight just for us. The day had been overcast with a drizzle of fine mist, but as we pulled up to the church, the sun burst forth in celebration. Daddy gave me one last, reassuring squeeze. We stepped into the church and into a new life for me. It was my wedding day.

I clutched Daddy's arm tightly as we walked down the aisle of that picturesque church. I heard him say, "Her mother and I do" as he answered the question "Who gives this woman to be married to this man?" and then I was exchanging rings with my new husband—rings in which were inscribed the words: "The same Spirit says the same thing."

God's Encouragement in Hard Places

~ Gigi ~

Stephan, the children, and I lived for a time outside Paris, in a big old house that looked as if it could have come right out of a Brontë novel. The large, drafty, three-story house was heated by a coal furnace way down in the basement—a furnace that had to be stoked every morning and every evening.

One day the fire in the furnace went out when Stephan was not home. I couldn't get it started again. Suddenly, I became very appreciative of heat. I wrote in my journal:

> Thank you, Father, for allowing me to be cold. We had to bundle up and sit around the little fireplace that wouldn't burn,

either, and we were cold. Thank you, because if we were always warm, we would never know the suffering of those who are always cold. Thank you because we did have warm clothes to put on and warm food to eat. Thank you for the coffee, tea, and hot chocolate. Thank you for this little experience. But most of all, thank you that once again we have heat.

At another time in our lives, we lived in the Middle East. One day friends came to visit. They noticed that even though I had a small baby, I had no washing machine. There were no disposable diapers either, and I had to do all the laundry, including cloth diapers, by hand. I'd boil them on the stove and then rinse and rinse and rinse them to make sure the soap was all out. I had no dryer, either; I hung them out in the desert dust to dry.

Our friends went back to the States and told my mother all about it. Her mother-heart was torn. On the one hand she wanted to help me—to sympathize with me—but on the other hand she wanted to encourage me.

She wrote:

My darling daughter,

I am so sorry that things are a bit difficult. I know that it is not easy to live where you are living. I know that it is sometimes difficult to care for your family as you would like. That it is hard to wash and iron and clean and cook in circumstances far different from your upbringing. But I am so grateful that the Lord has given you good health and the strength with which to work. I am so grateful that he has given you a husband and babies to care for. I am so grateful that he has given you soap and water with which to wash, and hands with which to scrub.

I love you,
Mother

Often encouragement, with a sense of perspective, is the best gift we can give someone.

Every Little Bit Helps

~ Gigi ~

"Mama, that's a pretty dress you have on," six-year-old Antony remarked as we started out the door.

"Oh, thank you, Honey," I replied.

I felt warm all over. I had glanced in the mirror earlier and been upset by the number of gray hairs that seemed to have suddenly appeared. I had also noticed a few more lines around my eyes and mouth, and thought that my dress fit a bit more snugly than it did a few months ago. To tell you the truth, I was feeling every bit of my middle-aged years ... until Antony told me he liked my dress. Funny how a simple remark from a six-year-old can transform one. For the rest of the day, I felt good about myself.

It reminded me of something Mother shared with her journal some years ago.

Dear Journal:

Never let a single day pass without saying an encouraging word to each child. Particularly wherever you have noticed any—even the slightest—improvement on some weak point— some point at which you have been hen-pecking and criticizing.

In David's prayer for Solomon, he said, "prayer also shall be made for him continually; *and* daily shall he be praised" (Psalms 72:15, KJV).

Someone wrote, "More people fail for lack of encouragement than for any other reason."

In a Little White Room

⇜ Gigi ⇝

I loved the little room I shared with my sister Anne. It was white, with a lovely bay window where the rhododendron bushes outside snuggled up so close you could almost reach out and touch their soft pink blossoms. Just beyond, the mountains towered so high we had to lean way down or go outside to see the top of the ridge called "Rainbow."

I slept in a big white bed. It really wasn't so very big; it was just that I was so small. We had two closets, one on each side of the room. The closet on the right was special, because high above it—out of reach—was a small cupboard where Mother would keep special treats. (These were confiscated from birthdays and Christmases when we were inundated with toys, and saved for sick-in-bed days.) Once, when I hurt my finger and had to have stitches, Mother reached in and found a lovely new baby doll for me.

When I was four, I became so ill that even the surprise from the hidden cupboard didn't make me feel any better. Mother was concerned and watched me closely. One day she came into my little room and sat down on the edge of the bed. She lovingly stroked my burning forehead and said, "God loves you very much, Gigi—so much that he sent his Son, Jesus, to die on the cross for you."

Then she repeated once again the story I had heard many times before. She explained how Jesus had been beaten and spit upon, and that although he had done nothing to deserve such treatment, he had taken that cruel punishment for me. He had even been nailed to a cross and left to die, and by taking our sins—our "badness"—on himself, he was making it possible for us to live with him forever in heaven when we die. She told me that even if I, Gigi Graham, had been the only little girl in the whole world, God would still have sent his Son to die—just for me.

"Gigi." Mother's voice was very gentle. "If you wish, you could ask Jesus to come into your heart right now."

Oh, how I wanted to do just that! So in simple, childlike faith I opened my heart to him and he came in—forgiving my "badness." I certainly didn't understand the theological implications of that moment, nor did I experience much emotionally. But I felt clean … and very much loved.

That day long ago, in my little upstairs bedroom, God began something in my life. And he isn't through with me. He continues to shape and mold me, adding his finishing touches.

Have you personally met Jesus Christ? Are you confident of your relationship with him? He's as near you right now as he was near to me in that little white room in the mountains.

You, too, are very much loved.

Just to Abide

✤ Gigi ✤

I could see the first rays of light as the sun made its way slowly up Little Piney Ridge. Only a few more minutes and it would burst forth, ushering in another day. Until then, I would sit at my window and savor these quiet moments.

Early-morning fog still covered most of the sleepy valley below, obscuring the little town of Black Mountain that was just beginning to stir. But the tops of the Blue Ridge Mountains stood out dark and clear against the dawn. And just beneath my window, the lilac bush was heavy with dew, its large fragrant blossoms bowed with the moisture's weight. They seem poised in anticipation of a new day. It promised to be a glorious one!

I prayed fervently, *O Lord, please let this be the day you and I get it together!*

After reading a portion of my Bible, I prayed again, giving the Lord my day. I felt so good. It was all so beautiful. Surely I wouldn't blow it today. I bounded down the stairs, inhaling the heavenly aroma of bacon and eggs emanating from the kitchen.

I tried. I really did. But my spirituality didn't even make it all the way through breakfast. First I argued with one of my sisters, then I talked back to my mother when she scolded me. Then, when I realized what I had done, I became so discouraged, I just gave up on that day completely.

So goes the story of my life. Trying so hard … and falling so short. I am a struggler. I'm always struggling to arrive at this or that spiritual plateau. I'm always wishing I could eliminate this or that problem or weakness. *If I could*, I think, *then I would be "worthy."* Living the Christ-like life just hasn't come easily for me. But I have a deep longing and desire to be like him that started in my childhood, continued into my teens, and followed me into my marriage.

Several years after this failed attempt at spirituality, I was sitting at another window overlooking another valley. By this time I was married to Stephan and living in Switzerland. I had been reading one of the many books on victorious Christian living that fill my shelves. As I gazed out over the flowered meadows to the snow-capped Alps beyond, I suddenly found tears streaming down my cheeks. I cried out in utter frustration at my same old problem. "But Lord! How? How? How?"

As I sat there with my bowed head in my hands, I remembered something I had read years before: "His Father said, 'Leave *that* book and read *the* Book that thou lovest best. Thou wilt find it much simpler'" (Amy Carmichael).

Perhaps I had been reading too many books about becoming a spiritual person. Perhaps I was trying too hard. My heavenly Father reminded me that I was created not to *be*, but to *belong*. For a moment I reveled in the thought. I don't have to be always positive, always smiling, always "up" as the books indicated—but I could rest in him and in his Word alone. It seemed too good to be true!

But it *is* true. Our part of becoming truly spiritual is to *abide,* to focus on belonging to him, and he will take care of the rest. As Corrie ten Boom used to say, "We need to quit struggling and start snuggling."

Sweet Treats from the Graham Family

⇒ Ruth and Gigi ⇐

What is coffee without a sweet treat to accompany it? Here are some of our favorite recipes.

AT LEFT:
Ruth and Gigi share
a joyful moment.

Our Favorite Chocolate Chip/Oatmeal Cookies

(Great with coffee!)

1/2 c. butter

1/2 c. vegetable shortening

1 c. light brown sugar

1 c. granulated sugar

2 eggs

1 t. salt

1 t. baking soda

1 t. vanilla

2 c. flour

2 c. quick-cooking oatmeal

1/2 package (6-ounce size) chocolate chips

Cream butter, shortening, and sugars together. Then beat in the eggs. Add salt, soda, vanilla, and flour. Then mix in oatmeal and chocolate chips. Bake at 350° for 10 to 12 minutes.

Ruth's Chocolate Sauce

(This is addictive!)

1 c. granulated sugar

1 c. corn syrup

1 c. cream

2 squares of bitter chocolate

pinch of salt

dash of vanilla

In a saucepan, cook until it is sticky.

Test it on ice cream to see if it is ready. (This is the fun part—keep on testing, and testing, and testing.)

Then spoon it over ice cream and eat (if you have any appetite after testing so much).

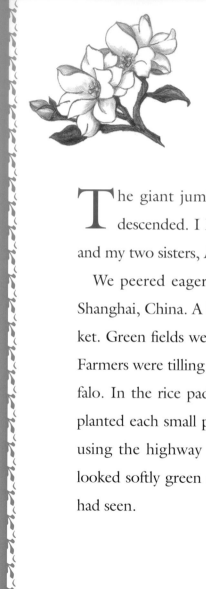

Roots

❧ Gigi ☙

The giant jumbo jet eased down through the clouds as it slowly descended. I had flown halfway around the world with my mother and my two sisters, Anne and Ruth, for this moment.

We peered eagerly from the windows, catching our first glimpse of Shanghai, China. A light gray fog covered the countryside like a soft blanket. Green fields were dotted by small and simple gray stone farmhouses. Farmers were tilling the soil with wooden plows pulled by large water buffalo. In the rice paddies, bent backs were all that was visible as workers planted each small plant by hand. Others were threshing wheat by hand, using the highway as a threshing floor. From the air, the countryside looked softly green and picturesque, resembling the many photographs I had seen.

The large plane continued its descent, and suddenly its tires screeched against the runway. We stepped off the plane and onto Chinese soil for the first time. In some strange way, we felt that we had been there before. It all seemed so familiar.

This was the land of Mother's birth, the land where she had spent the first seventeen years of her life. We climbed into a minivan and began what was to be the first of many thrilling (in more ways than one) rides in China. Our driver had a unique way of zooming through the crowded streets at top speed, never letting up on the horn and seldom touching the brakes. Miraculously, he avoided hitting anyone.

As dusk began to settle that first evening, a little maid came in to turn down the beds and close the drapes in our hotel room. I asked her to please leave the curtains open so I could watch the lights come on in the city. But as darkness fell, the city was cloaked with utter blackness, dotted only here and there by a few dim lights.

Fourteen million people and so little light, I thought, and I thought too of a Scripture, "And there was thick darkness in all the land" (Ex. 10:22, RSV).

As we traveled during the following days, this verse took on even more meaning. We discovered not only physical darkness in the land, but spiritual, economic, and political darkness as well.

From Shanghai, we traveled two days by train, van, and ferry, crossing the Grand Canal and then heading north to Huai Yin, where Mother had been born and where our grandparents had served as medical missionaries for more than twenty-five years. This trip took us to more than a dozen cities in eighteen days, cities that reminded us of our heritage and God's faithfulness.

On Mother's Day, in the city where Mother was born, we awoke to glorious sunshine and deep-felt emotions. We toured what is left of the hospital compound where God had done so many miracles and changed so many lives through the ministry of our grandparents. We met many whose lives had been touched physically and spiritually by faithful missionaries.

I couldn't keep back the tears as I thought of my grandfather, working tirelessly and unselfishly for these people he loved, even giving them his own blood when needed. Grandfather was always quick to point out that although he could help heal their bodies, eventually their bodies would die; their souls were of much more importance. He told them of the love of Jesus.

My grandparents were fun-loving Christians who were deeply committed to one another and to their work. They realized their total dependence upon Almighty God and his grace and mercy. As we traveled, we recalled some of the stories we had been told as children—stories of God's protection, of his loving care and concern.

When our aunt was a small child in China, she asked one Christmas for doll baby glasses. My grandmother wondered how in the world she would ever be able to fulfill such a request. But the next box of missionary donations to arrive from America contained—you guessed it—a pair of doll baby glasses. Hearing that story recounted had always touched us with the tenderness of a loving heavenly Father who cared about a little girl's request in faraway China.

We visited the small stone house where Mother was born more than seventy years ago. I thought of my grandmother, giving birth in that small room with my grandfather tenderly caring for her.

I thought of the years of Mother's teaching and living a personal, vibrant faith. I longed to be alone with my mother and sisters to let all of these emotions flow, but in China, with more than a billion people, it is nearly impossible to be alone. So I pondered in the privacy of my own heart. I thought of how often God told the children of Israel to "remember."

"Remember what the Lord thy God did ...," "Remember how the Lord led ...," and "Remember the days of old; consider the generations long past. Ask your father and he will tell you, your elders, and they will explain to you" (Deut. 32:7).

I came home to America and to my family with a new desire and a new determination to be not only as faithful as I can be in my own life, but to faithfully tell my children of all that God has done and is doing. I want to remind them, encourage them, and tell them again and again of the faithfulness of our God.

Remember the days of old; consider the generations long past. Ask your father and he will tell you, your elders, and they will explain to you.

DEUTERONOMY 32:7

The Lamplighter

~ Gigi ~

I could see my breath white against the cold darkness as I trudged up the steep hill to our chalet. The familiar tinkling of the cow bells from the surrounding hillside pastures soothed and comforted me.

The weather had suddenly turned colder. *The snow will not be far away tonight,* I thought to myself. Tomorrow the mountain peaks would be dressed in a fresh, clean layer of white. I knew that soon the cows would be snuggled into barns for the winter months and the swish, swish sound of brightly dressed skiers speeding by on the hillsides would replace the sound of cowbells.

I looked up at the star-studded night sky. So many thousands of bright, white points of light. Each one cut a tiny hole in the darkness. As I walked, I remembered a story.

Many years ago in England, a small boy sat in his nursery window watching the lamplighter light the gas-burning streetlamps along the road in front of his home.

His mother called him to come get ready for bed. When he didn't respond, she called again. After the third attempt, she went to look for him. She found him staring out of the window and asked, "Son, what are you looking at?"

"Oh," replied the child, "I am watching the man put holes in the darkness."

On the Swiss mountain, under the dark, star-strewn sky, I thought, *this is exactly what the Lord does for us.* Jesus is Light. He did not come to take away all our pain and suffering, nor even to explain it, but he came to be with us in our pain and suffering. He is present with us, and his light puts holes in the darkness of our lives.

Tonight the Lights Went Out

Tonight
the lights went out
(aftermath of sudden storm).
Trapped in the dark
I groped about
to light candles
and a fire
to keep me warm,
wondering how
men manage who
have no fire, no candlelight
to company them
some stormy night.

Ruth

Am I Going to Heaven

❧ Gigi ❧

One Friday afternoon, when I was a very small girl, Mother promised to take Anne, Ruth, and me to our one-room mountain cabin to spend the night.

When we arrived home from school, Mama had everything all packed. After changing into play clothes, we piled into the Jeep. Soon we were bouncing along the old dirt road that climbed steeply upward to the small one-room cabin.

After a supper of hot dogs and hot chocolate prepared over the open fire, we sat on the porch, reading and talking until dark. Then suddenly I asked a question that had been troubling me all afternoon.

"Mama, if I die, will I go to heaven?" I had good reason to ask, for that very afternoon, for the umpteenth time, I had been punished for teasing my little sister.

"You tell me," she replied.

"I don't know."

"Do you want me to tell you how you can know?"

"I don't think you can know for sure."

"Oh, yes, you can."

"How?"

"First," she explained, "you know that you are a sinner, don't you?"

"Of course!" There was never any doubt about *that*. I always seemed to be getting into trouble.

"Then you confess your sins to the Lord."

"I've done that," I nodded. "After I got so mad this afternoon, I told him I was sorry three times—just in case he didn't hear me the first time."

"He heard you the first time," Mama said. "You are a child of God because you asked Jesus into your heart. Do you remember being born into God's family when you were only four?"

"No," I shook my head. "I don't remember it. I only know what you've told me. And I'm still not sure I'm going to heaven."

"Gigi, just because you can't remember the day doesn't make it any less real." Her voice became stern for a moment. "Would you call God a liar?"

"Of course not!" I protested.

"But that's just what you're doing," she insisted. "He tells us that if we confess, he will forgive [1 John 1:9]. If we believe, we have eternal life [1 John 2:25]. You have confessed and you believe—yet you don't think God will keep His promise? That's the same as calling him a liar."

She paused a moment for me to reflect on her words. "Don't you recall what John 3:16 says? Recite it for me."

I repeated the familiar, much-loved verse: "For God so loved the world, that he gave his only begotten Son that whosoever believeth in him should not perish, but have everlasting life" (KJV).

Then Mama held up a piece of paper and said, "Whoever wants it can have it."

I snatched it from her fingers.

"What makes you think I said *you*?" Mama demanded.

"You said, 'whoever.'"

"Exactly."

We knelt by the cabin's bed and prayed for assurance.

"Mama," I said breathlessly as we rose to our feet, "I feel like a new person."

The next day, this "new person" scampered down Assembly Drive to the Montreat gate and uprooted a dozen water lilies that had just been planted in time for the arrival of the season's first tourists and conferees. Mama escorted me to the town manager's office with the evidence wilting in my tight little fist, my face pale as I worried aloud that I was going to be thrown into jail. (And Mama said nothing to dispel the fear.)

I confessed and apologized. With so much practice, I was a good little "repenter."

That night as Mama tucked me into bed, I asked plaintively, "Have I been good enough today to go to heaven?"

"Now, how much," Mama wrote in her diary that night, "should I impress on Gigi the doctrine of salvation by grace when, really, for a child of her disposition, one could be tempted to think that salvation by works would be more effective?"

That was not the last time I was plagued with doubts, because "being good" has been harder for me than for some. The devil loves to make me feel unworthy of God's love and grace. But the Scriptures clearly teach that his love is unconditional, and that salvation is by grace alone, and is not dependent on my performance or feelings.

For that, I will be eternally grateful.

Above the clouds
thick, boiling, low,
appear the peaks
she came to know
as Father, Son
and Holy Ghost;
often when she
sought them most,
they would be hid
in clouds from view.
Distraught by cares
she always knew,
silent, unseen
they still were there,
like God himself—

unchanged, serene.
Knowing this,
she gathered strength
for each day's journey—
length by length.

Written by Ruth for Gigi
when Gigi lived in Switzerland

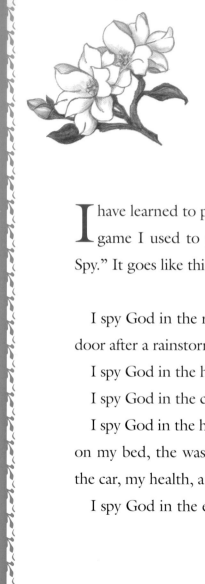

I Spy

~ *Gigi* ~

I have learned to play a type of spiritual observation game much like the game I used to play with the kids on long car trips, the game of "I Spy." It goes like this:

I spy God in the raindrops clinging to the petals of the rose outside my door after a rainstorm.

I spy God in the healthy birth of my child.

I spy God in the check that I am able to write for the groceries.

I spy God in the hot water that comes out of the faucet, the clean sheets on my bed, the washing machine that cleaned them, the full gas tank in the car, my health, a good night's rest, a good meal, and a full stomach.

I spy God in the example of older, faithful saints, like my grandparents,

my teachers, pastors, and friends who have faithfully taught me and prayed for me.

I spy God in the beauty of a sunset over the Everglades, in the majesty of the snow-covered Alps, in the gentle lapping of the surf upon the shore, in the softness of a spring shower and the awesomeness of a summer thunderstorm.

I spy God in the sticky kiss of a child, the hug of a teenager, the note from a grown son, the Mother's Day card, the reassuring pat from my husband as he passes by.

I spy God in the words of a child.

I spy God in my grandson's excited eyes when I suggest that we go get ice cream.

I spy God in remembering his faithfulness.

I spy God in his mercy and grace each and every day.

I spy God everywhere.

Why?

❧ *Ruth* ❧

There are times when the question "why?" is literally wrenched from a person—even an earnest believer.

When I was a child, one of our missionaries committed suicide. Overworked and under unbearable pressure, this dear Christian broke.

And there was the time Uncle Ed and Aunt Gay Currie's little John Randolph—left briefly unattended—fell into a tub of scalding laundry water. Not too long after this, their little daughter, Lucy Calvin, ate poisonous beans and died.

Uncle Jack Vinson, who wrote to inform the larger mission family of the tragedy, told of going to comfort Aunt Gay (Uncle Ed was away in the countryside at the time), and of returning, having been comforted by her instead.

Little did we know how short the time would be until Uncle Jack himself would be killed by bandits. That time, it was Uncle Ed who went out and retrieved his body. Not only had he been shot, but he had been beheaded as well.

Another "why?" happened when I was in high school in Korea. One night a fellow student was killed by a train. It threw a pall over the entire student body.

So down through life from time to time, the cry of our anguish goes up to God, "Lord, take away the pain!"

Franklin, our older son, and his flight instructor were once miraculously saved from a plane crash. Then the next year, this same instructor was killed in another plane crash.

The Billy Graham Evangelistic Association's team "family" has not been exempt. One son was accidentally shot by his cousin. A daughter was left a vegetable from illicit drugs. An ideal son died on the operating table.

There have been unexplained suicides, broken marriages, runaways....

Is it wrong to ask why? I wondered.

Turning to my concordance, I began to look up Bible references. In Exodus 5:22 Moses asked, "Why?"

And God's only answer was, "Now you will see what I will do" (Ex. 6:1).

Even our Lord asked, "Why?" when he hung on the cross.

Someone has said that faith never asks why. But surely, when pushed beyond endurance, one often cries, "Why?"

I believe, like a character in Elie Wiesel's novel *Night*, we must "pray for courage to ask the right questions."

You might get some interesting answers. But if God chooses to remain silent, faith must be content.

I Lay My Whys

I lay my "whys"
before your Cross
in worship kneeling,
mind too numb
for thought,
heart beyond
all feeling.

And worshiping,
realize that I,
knowing you,
don't need a "why."

⇜ *Ruth* ⇝

Fertilizer for a
Beautiful Character

⚹ Gigi ⚹

Even if suffering is caused by the wrongdoing of others, so was our Lord's. Even if there is no explanation, we accept and worship and humbly acknowledge that a sovereign, loving God does not have to answer all of our questions or give a reason for all that he does or allows into our lives.

Someone once said, "Christ didn't come to take away all pain and suffering, nor did he come to explain it, but he came so that he might go through it with us."

Triumphant suffering is a wonderful fertilizer for a beautiful character. Some of the most beautiful Christians I know have suffered much.

Just as the lapidarian, after careful examination of an uncut gemstone, delivers a sharp, skillful blow to it in order to enhance its beauty and increase its value, so the Lord allows blows to come to us.

As the faithful gardener carefully cuts and prunes in order that his garden may be more beautiful, healthy, and productive, so the Lord must at times prune us to bring out our character and faith.

Jill Briscoe was once doing a study on vines and vineyards. In her research on pruning she learned, to her amazement, that pruning is necessary to restore a weather-beaten vine, to enhance the beauty of the vine, to give the health to the vine, to increase the vigor and production in an old vine, to remove weak parts of the vine, and to let the sunshine in to other parts of the vine. What a beautiful analogy!

Some of us are weather-beaten. We need restoring. Some of us have been Christians for a long time, and now we need a new sense of vigor and purpose. Unnecessary weights that have weakened us need to be removed. Some of us need to endure pruning in order for others to be able to see the Son. The pruning is never for punishment, but for strength, beauty, health, and service.

If for some reason God has appointed you special trials, special burdens, special weights, rest assured that in his heart, he has also reserved a very special place for you.

Hudson Taylor once said, "Never mind how great the pressure is, only where the pressure lies. Never let it come between you and the Lord. Then the greater the pressure, the more it presses you to his heart."

Often the weight we carry is the anchor for our lives. It anchors us to the Lord Jesus. It keeps us dependent on him and his strength.

In the Desert but Not Deserted

ᵔ Gigi ᵔ

There has been a hot dry wind blowing for several days now, unusual for our tropical climate. It reminds me of the times in my life when I feel as though a dry wind has blown upon me both spiritually and emotionally.

That's when, I, too, feel dry, parched: just like the grass and plants must feel this week. Sometimes I just don't feel spiritual. I don't feel like praying. I am in desperate need of water, yet I have little or no desire to read my Bible, which would quench my thirst. Sometimes I even question my salvation. I become concerned. If I were truly in love with Jesus, wouldn't I feel it and want to spend as much time with him as possible?

My tendency in drought is to pretend, to wear a mask to hide my dryness and my lack of spiritual desire. But soon it becomes evident that I am not what I should be.

Often it is in times like this that I find that I need the Lord the most. When I *feel* like reading my Bible and praying, I probably don't need it as much as when I don't feel like it. So, discipline plays a part and although I try not to worry about my dry condition, I also try to find small springs of water: a devotional book of encouraging words, a verse to meditate upon, a quiet walk when I can talk to the Lord, honestly expressing myself— after all, he knows all about me anyway. It's so wonderful just to be able to be myself with him.

During my desert times, I try not to sit around lamenting my lack of feelings, nor do I try to arouse my feelings. I simply wait in faith.

Over the years, I have discovered that feelings are often the devil's counterfeit for faith. They come and go much like the feelings in marriage. Sometimes I feel in love, other times I feel little or nothing, but that doesn't change the fact that I am married. Even though my feelings fluctuate, my marriage status is still secure.

I have also discovered that blessings and opportunities abound in desert places. In the desert, Moses found a burning bush; Hagar, springs of water to quench her thirst; Jacob, a host of angels climbing a ladder and a special relationship with God. In the desert, an angel appeared to Elijah, ministered to him, encouraged him, and even cooked a meal for him. In the desert Philip found a man who needed a Savior.

So, in my desert I have come to accept my position in Christ as sure and secure, because it has *nothing* to do with me and *everything* to do with him.

Mother too has felt this wind. She once wrote:

Oh …
we are dry.
The grass is brown,
the flowers dwarfed,
the garden droops—
All parched plants are hanging down;
this evening angry clouds
hang low—
the air is still,
no storm winds blow,
and no birds sing;
a pall hangs over
everything.
Then
came the rain:
heavy, silent, brief—
no thunder and no lightning
but, Oh the relief!

P.S. Lord I am dry.
Ruth

Please Pray I'll Catch a Lizard

⚘ *Ruth* ⚘

I was alone in the kitchen, catching up on the mail, when I came across a very serious request written to The Samaritan's Purse ministry from a very serious four-year-old supporter.

"… and please pray I'll catch a lizard."

I laughed out loud. I loved it!

I thought of Murdock, the giant gray lizard who lives in the old hew logs outside the bay window of our bedroom, and of Matilda, his somewhat-smaller wife.

One October morning, a baby lizard had crawled up to the topmost log of those stacked beneath the bedroom window and stared solemnly at me. I stared back, not quite so solemnly. Soon he scrambled off. That brief, lighthearted moment brightened my day. So I, too, can appreciate lizards.

Only the day before I sat in my kitchen reading this four year old's request, I had been in Paris, where I was with Bill for Mission France. There had been much prayer all over France on behalf of those who might

be unfulfilled spiritually and stifled materially—and here was a small boy praying for a *lizard!*

But the God, who so graciously answered our prayers for France, cared about the concern of one small boy for a lizard. Not once has God ever said, "Don't bother me. Can't you see I'm busy?"

No, each person is special to him, he who calls every star by name, who has numbered the hairs of our heads, and who knows the number of grains of sand on the ocean shores. I am sure that a small boy's request for a lizard would be duly noted. In fact, I imagine the angels themselves enjoyed that small request with, perhaps, angelic chuckles.

I remembered reading a little poem:

> And then a little laughing prayer
> Came running up the sky,
> Above the golden gutters, where
> The sorry prayers go by.
> It had no fear of anything.
> But in that holy place.
> It found the very throne of God
> And smiled up in his face.

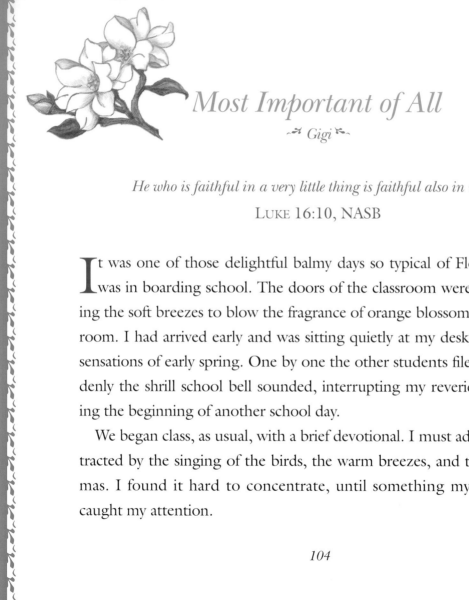

Most Important of All

~ Gigi ~

He who is faithful in a very little thing is faithful also in much.

LUKE 16:10, NASB

It was one of those delightful balmy days so typical of Florida where I was in boarding school. The doors of the classroom were open, allowing the soft breezes to blow the fragrance of orange blossoms through the room. I had arrived early and was sitting quietly at my desk, savoring the sensations of early spring. One by one the other students filed in and suddenly the shrill school bell sounded, interrupting my reverie and indicating the beginning of another school day.

We began class, as usual, with a brief devotional. I must admit I was distracted by the singing of the birds, the warm breezes, and the sweet aromas. I found it hard to concentrate, until something my teacher said caught my attention.

"The only thing the Lord requires of us," she was saying, "is faithfulness."

I felt both excitement and peace at those words. There, sitting at my school desk in central Florida, a huge weight was lifted from my shoulders. Because, you see, even at my tender age, I had been feeling an awesome responsibility to "measure up." There was so much to live up to, so many *big* footsteps to walk in, so many examples to follow that I just didn't see how I was going to do it!

But if the Lord's only requirement of me was faithfulness, then *he didn't expect me to be like anyone else!* And if the importance was in my faithfulness and not in the "greatness" of my task, then with his help I could serve and please him in my own unique way. What a comfort! From that day on, my prayer was that no matter what he gave me to do— whether great or small, public or private, I would be faithful.

For me, faithfulness has meant staying up all night with a sick child, pressing my husband's suits when he forgets to take them to the cleaners, washing windows, and pulling weeds, to name a few things. For others, it may mean remaining in a mundane or monotonous job or in a behind-the-scenes ministry.

Not everyone possesses boundless energy or a conspicuous talent. We are not equally blessed with great intellect or physical beauty or emotional strength. But we have all been given the same ability to be faithful. And as we are told in the parable of the talents, it is our faithfulness that receives the commendation of God: "Well done, good and faithful servant! You have been faithful with a few things; I will put you in charge of many things" (Matt. 25:21).

Many years have passed since my teacher shared this simple truth with us, but it continues to be a source of encouragement to me even now. I still tend to compare myself to others. And sometimes when I see those gifted Christians who seem to achieve so much for the Lord, I am tempted to admonish myself: *Gigi, if they can do it, so can you! After all, look at the advantages you have had!* Then I recall that balmy day so long ago and hear my Lord saying to me: "I am not requiring all this of you. You have placed these pressures and expectations on yourself. I ask only that you be faithful."

The little things that bug me,
resentments deep within;
the things I ought to do, undone,
the irritations one by one
till nerves stretch screaming-thin
and bare for all the world to see—
which needs His touch to make it whole
the most, my body or my soul?

I pray—but nothing comes out right,
my thoughts go flying everywhere;
my attitudes are all confused,
I hate myself—I am not used
to hands all clenched, not clasped, in prayer,
and heart too leaden to take flight;
which, oh, which, needs to be whole
the most, my body or my soul?

I cannot read. I cannot pray.
I cannot even think.
Where to from here? And how get there
with only darkness everywhere?
I ought to rise and only sink …
and feel His arms, and hear Him say,
"I love you" … It was all my soul
or body needed to be whole.

Ruth

*Written for Gigi when she was living
in Europe and going through a very difficult time.*

The Vital Constant

Ruth

As I grow older and look back over my life, the one constant that I can see is "faithfulness."

Not my faithfulness, which was distracted or diverted too often, but God's faithfulness.

Better Than I Thought

~ Gigi ~

Now unto him that is able to keep you from falling, and to present you faultless
before the presence of his glory with exceeding joy …

JUDE 24, KJV

The story is told of a certain Italian painter who lost some of his artistic skill as he grew older. One evening he sat discouraged before a canvas he had just completed. He was painfully aware that it didn't burst with life as had his former paintings. As he climbed the stairs to bed, his son heard him mumbling to himself, "I have failed. I have failed."

Later that evening the son, also an artist, went into the studio to look at his father's painting. He, too, noticed that something was missing. Taking the palette and brush, he set to work, adding a touch of color here, a shadow there, a few highlights, greater depth. He continued far into the night, until at last the canvas fulfilled the old master's vision.

When morning came, the aging artist entered the studio to examine the work once again. He stood amazed before the perfected canvas and exclaimed in utter delight, "Ah, I have wrought better than I thought!"

The day will come when we will look upon the canvas of our lives and through the transforming power of Christ—a few shadows, a bit of color, dramatic highlights, added depth—we will be amazed to discover that we too fulfill our Heavenly Father's original vision.

As Jesus steps up and presents each of us, faultless, before his throne, and we hear the Father's, "Well done, thou good and faithful servant," we, too, will exclaim with utter joy, "Ah, I have wrought better than I thought!"*

Take heart! Remember … it is not about us, but about his glory.

*Adapted from G.H. Morley, *A Quest for Serenity* (Nashville: Word, 1989), 66.